Once More

Once more it's yesterday. Once more I walk the road backward. Once more, like dim, distant music, I live the tears and laughter of other years.

Once more I trudge to Kinderschule, to Grade School, to Church — to sit on the very front bench under the stern scrutiny of the "Vorsteher", the Elders.

Once more, as a pre-teener I pick apples in the Communal Orchards, help with the harvest in field and garden.

Once more it is a long-gone May, and every yard and garden is a riot of pink and white. Once more, it is a far-away June, and on a moonlit night heavy with the scent of roses I kiss a girl and the world turns upside down.

Once more, in solemn procession, we escort grandparents and parents, friends and neighbors, to their final resting place in our quiet cemetery with its row on row of identical moss-coated, weather-beaten markers, where the winds sigh a lullaby through the sentinel pines and yews.

Once more . . . — *Henry Schiff*

Dedication, Acknowledgments

At one time, according to Historian Bertha Shambaugh in her book, *Amana That Was,* "personal photographs were severely condemned and absolutely forbidden." She reports that in 1873 "a form of idolatry which had crept in and had become frequent was severely attacked, and the annihilation or surrender of the respective objects was demanded. This was, namely, the custom of having photographs or pictures of one's own self taken which is already prohibited in the Ten Commandments, and which the Lord, moreover, had expressly forbidden in his testimonies, but which of late had nevertheless become very popular, especially among our own people."

As of 1900, Mrs. Shambaugh says, "Today, however, the ordinance against photographs is not strictly observed. Indeed, there is scarcely a sitting-room in the seven villages without an album which contains photographs not only of friends and relatives but many members of the Community who have had them taken on some holiday to the city."

Mrs. Shambaugh cites an old Amana saying which doubtless had been invoked: "Well, young people will be some foolish" and so "some things the elders must overlook."

This collection of pictures, illustrating the communal way of life they knew so well, is dedicated to the photographers in the Colonies who took most of these pictures — John L. Eichacker (1882-1935), Homestead postmaster; William Foerstner (1881-1974), manager of the High Amana store; Christian Herrmann, M.D. (1890-1970) of Middle Amana; F. William Miller (1876-1952), Amana pharmacist; Fred Oehl, Sr. (1866-1946), Amana carpenter whose photograph is on the cover; and Jacob Selzer (1888-1917), saddle maker at Homestead.

Another sensitive photographer whose work is included is J. Richmond of Cedar Rapids, Iowa.

The Amana Heritage Society assisted in the collection of these photographs and in editorial research. Many individuals also assisted. They include: Emaline Bendorf, Mathilda Benzinger, Erna Conrow, Louise DuVal, Alma Ehrle, Erna Fels, Emily Hahn, Louise Haldy, Johanna Herrmann, Emily Jeck, Dr. and Mrs. Henry Moershel, Marietta Moershel, Eva Noe, William Noe, Carl Oehl, Elsie Oehler, Fred and Marie Ruedy, Susanna Rettig, Madeline Roemig, Henry Schiff, Ruth Schmieder, Marie Schneider, Carl Selzer, Linda Selzer, Emma Setzer, Don Shoup, Lina Zierold, Connie Zuber and others, all of or from the Amanas; Sutherland Cook of Cedar Rapids; the State Historical Society of Iowa; the University of Iowa Photographic Service, and Fred W. Kent of Iowa City.

Photographs collected by Joan Liffring-Zug, Iowa City, Iowa. Text edited by John Zug. Graphic design by Esther Feske. Printed by Julin Printing Co.

Exhibition development in collaboration with L. G. Hoffman, Director, Davenport Art Gallery, Davenport, Iowa.

Cover: Communion Sunday in Amana Early 1900's.

Library of Congress Catalog Card Number: 74-26353.
ISBN 0-9603858-8-6
Third printing. 1981
Copyright, 1975, The Amana Society, Amana, Iowa 52203.
All rights reserved under International and Pan-American copyright conventions. Photographs may not be reproduced in any form without the written approval of Joan Liffring-Zug except as illustrations for a review of the book.

Published by Penfield Press
For more information on books about
Amana, write Penfield Press
215 Brown Street
Iowa City, Iowa 52240

The Amanas Yesterday

Amana about 1900 — kitchen gardens, homes, factories.

The Amanas Yesterday

It was in 1714 in southwestern Germany that two men founded a religious movement that later became known as the Community of True Inspiration and which today is the Amana community.

The ancestors of the present Amana people came to the United States beginning in 1842, building six villages in the vicinity of Buffalo, N.Y. — Middle Ebenezer, Upper Ebenezer, Lower Ebenezer and New Ebenezer in New York State and two villages in Canada.

Because the Buffalo area was being rapidly urbanized, the group sought land to the west, and in 1854 purchased the site of the present Amana Colonies.

After arrival in this country, the group adopted a religious-communal way of life, with all property held in common and with all church and secular decisions being made by the same leadership.

The communal way of life lasted nearly a century, until the people voted a separation of "church and state" in 1932 — effectively adopting the free enterprise way of life that surrounded them.

Purpose

The Constitution and By-laws of the Community of True Inspiration, incorporated in 1859 under the name of the Amana Society, stated in part:

"The purpose of our association as a religious Society is . . . no worldly or selfish one, but the purpose of the love of God in His vocation of grace received by us, to serve Him in the bond of union, inwardly and outwardly according to His laws and His requirements in our own consciences, and thus to work out the salvation of our souls, through the redeeming grace of Jesus Christ, in self-denial, in the obedience to our faith, and in the demonstration of our faithfulness in the inward and outward service of the Community, by the power of grace, which God presents us with.

"And to fulfill this duty we do hereby covenant and promise collectively and each to the other by the acceptance and signing of this present constitution.

"In this bond of union tied by God amongst ourselves, it is our unanimous will and resolution, that the land purchased here and that may hereafter be purchased, shall be and remain a common estate and property, with all the improvements thereupon and all appurtenances thereto, as also with all the labor, cares, troubles and burdens, of which each member shall bear his allotted share with a willing heart . . .

"Agriculture and the raising of cattle and other domestic animals, in connection with some manufactures and trades, shall under the blessing of God form the means of sustenance for this Society. Out of the income of the land and the other branches of industry the common expenses of the Society shall be defrayed.

"The surplus, if any, shall from time to time be applied to the improvement of the common estate of the Society, to the building and maintaining of meeting- and school-houses, printing-establishments, to the support and care of the old, sick and infirm members of the Society, to the founding of a business- and safety-fund, and to benevolent purposes in general."

Leadership

Christian Metz was the "Werkzeuge" or inspired leader who caused the people to leave Germany and settle in America. There has been no "Werkzeuge" since the death in 1883 of Barbara Heinemann Landmann at the age of 88.

The control and management of all the affairs of the Amana Society was vested in a board of trustees consisting of 13 members, elected annually out of the number of elders.

This election was held annually on the first Tuesday in December. Each male member who had signed the Constitution, and also the widows and such female members over 30 years of age, who were not represented by a male member, were entitled to vote.

Elders had been chosen by the "Werkzeuge", but since 1883 they have been nominated by the local "Bruderrath" or Council of Elders, and confirmed or rejected by the "Grosse Bruderrath" or Board of Trustees, also known as the Supreme Council.

Elders conducted the church services, and met each Sunday morning. The local Council of Elders met weekly, and the Supreme Council met once a month.

The local council ruled on local problems only. The elected Supreme Council or Board of Trustees ruled on both spiritual and temporal matters. Thus it set the dates for communion services, fast days, penitence services, etc. It also set the yearly allowance, paid not in cash but in credit at the various stores. This allowance varied from $35 to $75 per person, depending on the Society's current financial structure. The allowance was equal regardless of your work, status or capacity.

The "Grosse Bruderrath" approved or vetoed purchasing requests from shops, departments and plants. It also authored occasional letters of exhortation, encouragement, admonition, warning, etc., that were read at regular church services. — *Henry Schiff.*

Congregations

Children and their young parents worshipped together, and there were separate services for older people and the "in-betweens" — people in their 30's and 40's. At "Allgemeine" or combined services, children occupied the front row benches. Evening prayer meeting attendance by children was at the discretion of the parents.

After you were in the middle church, if you had more children you went back to the children's group. You had to stay back until the child was two years old. That was not necessarily a deterrent to having more children, but once you were in the second church, you liked to stay there. The services, however, were the same.

Sunday School was initiated in 1933. It was prompted by the adoption of an All English-No Religion curriculum at the Amana School System. Before 1933, a regular course of religion was part of the Amana school curriculum.

Amana Church Society

In six villages, the church was erected and in use in the year of the initial settlement. These dates were: Amana, 1855; West Amana and South Amana, 1856; High Amana, 1857; East Amana, 1860; Homestead, 1861. Middle Amana was settled in 1861, the church was first used in 1862.

Thus did the first settlers in the Colonies, urgently needing everything including even shelter from the elements, bespeak the importance of religion in their daily lives.

Regular services were 11 times each week — morning services Wednesdays, Saturdays and Sundays, afternoon services on Sundays, and evening prayer meetings each day. There were daily services during Holy Week, and other special services for Ascension Day, Pentecost, and the day after Christmas, New Year's Day and Easter.

Unpretentious, the churches were indistinguishable in appearance from the homes and other buildings. Inside, the white-washed walls, bare floors and unpainted benches were a testimony of the simplicity of the Christian faith.

Women, wearing black shawls and bonnets, sat on one side of the church, men on the other. There were no musical instruments. Hymns were sung, and the messages of the elders were from the Bible and from the testimonies of the founders and leaders of the church. They urged a peaceful, brotherly way of living in simple dignity and humility, faith in Christ and belief in the word of God.

Communion

Communion was biennial — every other year — and there were five separate Communion Services on successive Sundays: "das erste Liebesmahl" for the senior group; "das zweite Liebesmahl" for the second-ranking group; "das dritte Liebesmahl" for the third-ranking groups; "das vierte Liebesmahl" for the fourth-ranking or junior group, and "das Kinder-Liebesmahl" for the children.

A special communion bread, a long French bread type of loaf, was baked by the village baker the day before the service. The wine had been aged in huge casks four to five years.

Part of the service was a foot-washing ceremony in commemoration of Christ washing the feet of His disciples.

The Children's Communion was held at a communal kitchen. Instead of bread and wine, they were served coffee cake and hot chocolate, to impart the meaning and significance of communions in the children's future, and to give them a sense of belonging. An Elder expounded on the meaning of communion, and hymns were sung. — *Henry Schiff.*

Holidays

New Year's Day, Good Friday, Easter, Pentecost, Ascension Day, Thanksgiving Day and Christmas were full church holidays, with all activities — except worship — coming to a full and complete halt. Good Friday, Karfreitag, was a fast day.

After Thanksgiving you scheduled a date with the village baker to bake your Christmas cookies — Weihnachts-Keks. On the appointed day, you took your cookie doughs to the bakery, and in the old brick, wood-fired oven you baked a fantastic assortment of honey and molasses, Springerle and Marzipan, Schweizer-Batzen and Wiesbader Brot, and Amana's very own, never equaled, nut cookies.

Baecker-Kuchen, a yeast raised, milk, shortening, sugar, rose water coffee cake, baked by the village baker the night before a holiday, and served at the communal kitchens with hot chocolate, was an Easter and Christmas tradition.

Silvester-Abend, New Year's Eve, began with the Allgemeine Nachtgebet, the portentious New Year's Eve prayer meeting.

There was the fitful light from the wall-bracketed kerosene lamps. The dirge-like traditional New Year's Eve hymn. To ''come last'' meant a death in the family during the coming new year.

Then the traditional Silvester-Feier, the New Year's Eve party. Group celebrations and gatherings, some in communal kitchens, some in various shops, some in homes.

Entertainment ranged from reviving the old Silvester legends of supernatural happenings on other Silvester-Abende, to games and just conversation.

The feast, around 10 o'clock, was traditional — wieners from the village butcher; Rohgeroeste (raw fried potatoes), store cheese and crackers, and beer. — *Henry Schiff.*

Thanksgiving

On Thanksgiving Day there were services in the morning and in the afternoon and everybody went except the children — we had special services.

And then we worked in the kitchen on the chicken soup to be done for the time when everyone came home. Oh my, that was quite a responsibility to have that big broiler with chickens cooking away.

We'd have to get the rice ready in time, and get it cooked so it was nice. We had to bring the chickens out of the broth and pick the meat off the bones — no bones in there; it had to be done right. — *Emma Setzer.*

Christmas

On December 24, one and all quit work at noon. At home, the door to one special room was closed. There would be hustling and bustling from within — your parents trimming the tree and readying the gifts.

No tree was up before Christmas. No gift was packaged, but all were arranged open on the spotless white linen tablecloth under the tree.

There was the early dusk of December, and a barely touched supper, excited anticipation, and waiting. Finally, your Dad would disappear through the Magic Door — to light the candles on the tree.

We would all kneel and say a prayer to the Christ Child, and, finally, the Magic Moment when the Magic Door would open and we could all enter.

The ''Rund-Brenner'' or round wick kerosene table lamp, had been extinguished; the only light came from the candles on the tree. The tree was on the table, and the table was covered with white linen. The Christmas angel atop the tree nearly touched the ceiling, and the ornaments were freckled with candle wax of Christmases gone by.

Perhaps two dozen candles festooned the branches, but rapt eyes reflected at least a million. The mingled scent of fresh-cut pine and lit candles was a fairy-distilled perfume.

Underneath was the manger, the Christ Child, the Wise Men, the shepherds. Spread over the table were gifts (no ''store-bought'' wrapping tied with scarlet ribbons). Gifts were arranged in neat, orderly fashion. Always a book — ''Hansel and Gretel'' for the very young, ''Robinson Crusoe'' for the pre-teener.

There might be a sled or skates, dolls and farm sets, doll houses and ''Stein-Baukasten'' or stone building block sets. And always ''etwas Nuetzliches'' — something useful, and ''etwas zum Anziehen'' — something to wear — gloves and scarves, boots and shoes, mufflers and leggings.

Perhaps there was a set of ''Goldschnitt-Versammlungsbuecher'' — gilt-edged hymnal and Bible. There was an orange and an apple; pink, white and yellow marshmallow fish and bananas; chocolate covered marshmallow rats; chocolate-covered mice with pink candy eyes and string tails.

And always ''Schlutz-Kandy'' (hard candy), ''Deutsche Nuesse'' (English walnuts) and peanuts. Christmas Eve at Old Amana, the dream of things that were.

Christmas morning after church, and all through the day, there was a continuous round of visits to see ''what the others got.'' Then, finally, on the Zweite Weihnachtsfeiertag — the Second Day of Christmas — you were alone with your treasures. — *Henry Schiff.*

Christmas presents came from general stores in each village.

Evergreen boughs in holders decorated table tops for Christmas.

Leaving men's entrance of church at Amana. At right — Children hold the two books the people carry to church, the Bible and the Psalter-Spiel, containing hymns. These children were photographed ready to attend the last Holy Communion before the Great Change of 1932, which separated church and secular activities.

The Soul of Amana

Truly, the Church has been able to retain a position of prominence in Amana's heritage. It is "the Soul of Amana".

Gratefully may we acknowledge that it has not succumbed "in the hum and whirl of new activities and worldly interests". Its humility and simple sincerity is expressed not only in the unpretentious appearance of its century-old churches and in the solemn dignity of its services, but also in the plain similarity of the tombstones in the seven pine-shrouded village cemeteries.

All these have remained essentially untouched by the changing times, except for establishing a Sunday School in each village in 1931, and for the introduction of the English language in the church services in 1961. Thus this part of Amana's religious heritage has also been hopefully preserved for future generations. — *Henry Moershel, M.D.*

The People

The Amana pioneers were of Swiss, German and Alsatian ancestry seeking religious freedom in the New World.

This unique picture shows an Amana wedding procession on Aug. 22, 1907. Leading are the bride, Christine Gernand, and bridegroom, William Foerstner, one of the photographers to whom this book is dedicated. Foerstner placed his camera at a window in the attic of the church. Shutter was clicked at the right moment by a friend.

Trousseau

Each girl started her trousseau as early as she could stitch, and she would mark sheets and pillowcases with a monogram, and hem them nicely. If it was too rainy for garden work, and there was not a full morning of kitchen duties, probably she could squeeze out an extra hour or so.

They made shirts — you could call them shifts today — every bit handmade, handstitched, handsewn.

I remember one lady said, "I started knitting baby bonnets when I was 16 just to learn the art of it." And then, you know, she'd put it away and she'd say that was my first bonnet. And by the time she could do it real well, she had enough bonnets for her first baby.

Every girl wanted to do those things, they wanted knitted lace, and they wanted nice things. Boys knitted, too. We had grammar school until three and from three to five we had crochet and knitting.

My husband knitted, and his things were for sale. I didn't do anything that was sold. I just knitted for the family. I knitted stockings and socks from the very beginning to the top. I still knit socks and stoles and even ties for Christmas. — *Emma Setzer.*

Courtship

Well, you'd see each other somewhere and catch each other's eye. There were fences all along, you know, and sometimes the young men would be standing along the fences leaning against the post. Girls would go by and you'd catch each other's attention like any other young people would.

West Amana girls loved color and we in South were not supposed to wear loud dresses or anything like that, but some bonnets probably had a purple flower or something. Then we'd have those ties — ribbon instead of the same material, you know. One man later told me that when he first met his future wife, he said, "Well, you've got nice colorful ribbons."

There weren't any activities, like baseball games — that came later. But you could go for a walk together, and we did. West and South young people often would walk and meet on the bridge. One time we went skating way back in the timber, at a place called the Bend.

I don't know why, but it seems the South Amana girls were falling all the time, and one of the West Amana boys said, "Why don't you tie a broom to your back? You'd sweep the ice."

Many years later, this boy's father died, and when his mother mentioned her son, I said I didn't know him, and she said, "Of course you know him. Don't you remember when he told you to tie brooms to your backs and sweep the ice?" He had gone home and told his mother what he said, and she had remembered. — *Emma Setzer.*

Engagements

The young couple announced their intent to the local Bruderrath, or Council of Elders. After "due deliberation" the Council approved and the wedding date was set — always a full year later.

If both the young people lived in the same village, they were separated, one or the other being moved to another village. Some of those who were transferred became very home-sick.

The purpose and intent of the waiting period was to give the young people ample time to dwell on the seriousness of their forthcoming step, plus a hindrance to possible premarital passion.

But, in keeping with Amana's traditional dating custom — every Wednesday, Saturday and Sunday were "date nights" — the young lovers were able to meet three times a week.

Weddings

After the year was up, you verified the wedding date with the Bruderrath, or Council of Elders, the officiating elder was named, and the bridal pair made the rounds of the entire home village delivering personally their invitations to the reception. Guests from other villages also would be invited.

Only the "nahe Verwandte" — relatives up to and including second cousins, were asked to the church ceremony.

Preparations were extensive. The wedding wine — both red and white — had been made four or five years previously, in anticipation of a sometime wedding. The wedding beer was brewed six months before the event to insure proper aging.

Cakes — white, yellow, marble, chocolate, angel, nut — were baked by the hundreds by the bride and groom's home kitchens, and by friends, relatives and well wishers. Peach Kuchen was often a wedding treat.

Wedding gifts were always "etwas Nuetzliches" (something useful). They were taken to either the bride or groom's home, and would fill entire rooms.

On the wedding day, the bridal party — those attending the church ceremony — were luncheon guests at the bride's home kitchen where she served as a "Kuechen-Maedel", working as a kitchen helper, cook, etc.

The church ceremony included opening and closing hymns, scripture reading, a short sermon stressing the solemnity of the occasion, then the ceremony. There was no other music. No rings were exchanged.

At about 3 p.m., the invited guests would gather at the bridegroom's home for the celebration. Feasting on cakes and crackers, beer and wine, the guests would enjoy group singing, games by the younger set, and just plain visiting, until about 6 p.m.

Again the young couple were separated. They did not set up housekeeping until a full week after the wedding. Their home — a previously assigned apartment of two, three or four rooms — would be furnished during the week. And on the Thursday following the wedding the young lovers would finally be united. — *Henry Schiff.*

Family portrait: Grandmothers, aunts, parents and child on steps of a community kitchen in Middle Amana. Dress materials were from Amana Calico Print Factory.

Birthdays

Mixed emotions: For the young, joy and delight. As you grew older you were ever mindful of man's mortality and the fleeting days and years.

Your gift? Something fashioned by loving hands, or purchased out of a meager allowance. For a boy, perhaps a pocket knife like your dad's. For a girl, perhaps a "Ruestmesser" or paring knife, made at the village blacksmith's and a duplicate of what your mom used at the communal kitchen.

The celebration? No party. The only approach to organized birthday recognition was a possible after-hours get-together with fellow employees, etc.

If a man, you furnished some slices of "Store-Kaese" (store cheese) and crackers, a ring of bratwurst or bologna from the village butcher shop, and a bottle or two of home brewed beer. If a woman, your kitchen and garden staff would toast you with lemonade or Himbeersaft (raspberry juice) and perhaps that very special Amana delicacy, Open Faced Ground Cherry Pie.

If a child, some "Nachbarskinder" (neighbor kids), a slice of cake and some home-made raspberry juice.

If an adult, a day like any day. After the work day, friends, relatives, neighbors would drop in to offer "herzliche Glueckwuensche zum Geburtstag" — birthday greetings. They would share a glass of much cherished, left-over "Hochzeitswein" (wedding wine) and a slice of home-baked nut cake. — *Henry Schiff.*

Funeral Customs

When death neared, the dying were never alone. When the awesome final moment came, you met it with decency and dignity. You had a doctor by your side to mark your passing. Immediate family was in the same room. Aunts, uncles, cousins, etc., were in an adjoining room. A hymm would be read, and prayers said.

Loving hands prepared you for burial. You would lie in state in the room where you died in a casket custom-built for you at the village cabinet maker's. There would be a stream of people — your entire home village and many from other villages, to view the remains and extend their sympathy. Two of your closest friends would "hold a wake" on your final two nights on earth.

On the day of the funeral the family would be honored luncheon guests at the kitchen that had served your needs. The "Verwandte" (relatives) gathered at the family home an hour before the services. They wended their way to church in sequence, first the closest male kin, then the female relatives.

At the church entrances, everyone waited; no one would enter until the "Verwandte" (family) were seated. The service included funeral hymns, scripture, prayer and eulogy.

Back home a final farewell before the casket was closed by the village cabinet-maker. The Leichenwagen (hearse) was a somber black springwagon. The horses, black, were groomed to a satiny sheen, and were driven by the village "Gaeuls-Baas" — local farm manager. The casket was covered with a white linen sheet. Pallbearers were friends designated by the family.

The procession: first the pallbearers, next the church elders, then in strict sequence the male next of kin, relatives, friends, etc., then in identical sequence the female segment. Bringing up the rear, in the same sequence, the "Schulkinder", school children with their teachers. Whether summer or winter, all were on foot.

The graveside ceremony: a hymn, the coffin lowered, a few token shovels of earth, a final prayer, and the procession dispersed — some to linger among the memory-evoking white markers, some to ponder life's finality on their homeward trek.

The next morning the "Sterbezimmer", the death room, underwent a complete and thorough ritual housecleaning to banish all taint of death. — *Henry Schiff.*

Midwives

In the years before the Great Change (1932), there was one midwife for each village.

The baby was born at home. We didn't bring him home — he was born at home. You were not qualified as a full-fledged obstetrical nurse until you had delivered three babies by yourself. The mother and the baby and you were there, and the doctor if he got there, and the grandmother and the husband. I was a midwife for 25 years. — *Emma Setzer.*

Kinderschule

Mother and baby stayed at home until the child was two years old and went to Kinderschule.

The child would be in Kinderschule from 8 to 11, and then would be home for lunch with mother — at home, not at the communal kitchen. After lunch the child went to Kinderschule again.

The children stayed in Kinderschule until age 7, and the older ones helped take care of the younger ones. We had little two-wheeled wagons — little square box carts with wooden wheels — and if you were lucky enough you'd find a boy who pulled you around.

There were usually three women assigned to the children. Some years there were more, some years not so many, depending on how many of the smaller children there were.

They had the three cutest cradles in my Kinderschule and I do not know what became of them, but I remember so well seeing smaller children, and sometimes I'd rock them. One might sit up, and I'd push him back down, and rock. Those children would be two and I was four, probably.

Sometimes a child would escape under the fence and go home. My sister escaped with another girl once, and my uncle was running the transfer wagon from Upper South to Lower South and they saw him and waved, and he took them along. The girls were lost. — *Emma Setzer.*

School

Children went to school from age 7 to 14 or 15. School was held 5½ days a week the year around. There were breaks for weeding in the gardens and fields, harvesting of apples, potatoes and onions, etc.

School opened with prayer and Bible reading. The "three R's" of reading, writing and arithmetic were important. Instruction was in German, except that geography was in English because all the names on the maps were in English.

At mid-morning, two older women came to school with bread and molasses or corn syrup or a special treat of honey. There were daily knitting lessons for both boys and girls.

The teacher was also in charge of the orchard. He'd dismiss school and take the children into the orchard and we would pick up every apple.

The small ones and the half-rotten ones would go to the pigs. Others would go to the kitchen. There wasn't an apple lost, every apple was used.

When the kitchen staff was ready to dry apples, we would help. The children peeled them with an apple peeler that was new, and those that were able would peel them by hand.

Then they were cored, halved and washed and hauled to the little drying place and put on trays — the fire had to be hot — and those trays were pushed in.

At night at 9 or 9:30 my father and mother would go once more and turn the apples. Some were probably dry enough and they'd come out. And then the next day we'd go and take them off the trays and put them into paper-lined baskets and they were ready for storage for winter. Every village dried apples. — *Emma Setzer.*

Communal Kitchens

There was no cooking in the homes. Families ate in groups of 30 to 60 at communal kitchens. There were a number of these in each village, and each kitchen had its own large garden.

The day began at 4:30 a.m. when the hearth was lit — with one match. Water was heated for coffee, potatoes were fried, bread was sliced. Butter and milk were prepared for serving.

In the dining room, the tables had been set the night before. The bell for breakfast rang at 6 a.m. The mid-day meal was at 11:30, evening meal at 6:30. There were coffee breaks at 9 a.m. and 3 p.m.

There were separate tables for men and women. Grace was said before and after meals, and there was no talking during the meals. Families with small children or the ill or elderly carried food home in hinged or willow baskets.

The long tables were filled with food. Meals included soup, meats, potatoes and other vegetables, salads, sauerkraut and bread. When the men came from the factories for coffee break, there was bread and cheese, and often radishes, with the coffee.

The day ended with the girls and women doing the dishes, cleaning the kitchen, and setting the tables for the next day's breakfast, all tasks being completed efficiently so as not to be late for evening prayer meeting.

It was an honor to be a Kuechenbaas (kitchen boss). Her social stature was almost next to that of being an elder.

It was the duty of the Kuechenbaas to plan the meals, extra dishes and desserts, and to bake the weekly "Kuchen".

The Kuechenbaas purchased the supplies, and supervised the preservation of food supplies — the canning and drying of fruits and vegetables.

She allocated supplies to each family as needed, such as butter, milk, eggs, sugar and coffee cake.

The Kuechenbaas and her family lived in living quarters attached to the kitchen.

One kitchen in each village was designated for serving any tramps that came through. Another kitchen fixed lunch for the night watchman. In threshing season, every kitchen prepared noon meals for threshers.

Each kitchen had a long hearth which was wood heated, and a large bake oven. There were rows of pots and pans.

The long dry sink had two round wooden tubs on it, and a drain board. One tub was for washing dishes, the other to rinse them, and the drain board was for drying.

Whey was added to the dishwater to make it soft. An elderly lady usually washed the knives and forks and spoons separately. These were also cleaned at least twice a week with powdered brick or wood ashes to make them shiny.

A young belle.

An oma (grandma) in church dress.

Bringing home a food basket from community kitchen in Middle Amana on a snowy day. Baskets were prepared for the ill, the elderly, and those with small children. Dr. Christian Herrmann took this photo of his mother in 1915.

Busy People Doing Things Together

Families often snacked at home with food from communal kitchens' 9 a.m. and 3 p.m. coffee breaks. Here Amana people entertain "outside" visitors.

A communal kitchen. Hearth and oven are wood-burning.

People were rarely alone in the old Amanas.

Planting onion sets in High Amana kitchen garden in 1908.

Kitchen workers sorting spinach. Baskets are Amana-made.

Garden Helpers

Each kitchen had a coaster wagon to haul up the bushels of beans and tomatoes and cucumbers. We young girls washed the tomatoes and cucumbers. Two or three garden ladies picked them and brought them up from the gardens to the pump. There wasn't a cucumber put up that we didn't wash. We had them by the barrel.

Every kitchen had a handy man around and he'd do things that women couldn't do. He would work at splitting and piling of wood for our kitchen. He would mow around the kitchen and he would help bring those baskets full of vegetables for the garden ladies.

Everybody knew who was our kitchen lady and that another lady was the garden lady and she had helpers, one or two. Some with small children could stay home a little longer in the morning or go home a little earlier for lunch.

Every kitchen raised onions for sale in the fall. They shipped to Chicago from 300 to 800 sacks from each kitchen. The first garden lady would come and say, "This week we have to do the onions." Well, we'd find the day when there was not too much to do in the kitchen and we'd get up early and do an hour before breakfast of that day. That was it. Things just went like so. Nobody objected, nobody had a thing to say about it. It was nice.

Every kitchen had its own flock of chickens.

We dried kale in the woolen mill drier at Middle. The kale would go into wooden barrels and we'd store it in the attic to use for greens. There were plenty of grapes and apples and cherries. Once a year, probably for a holiday, we'd have peach Kuchen. — *Emma Setzer.*

Spring cleaning, 1915.

Spring Cleaning

Spring cleaning started with the first warm day of the new year, and was done one room at a time.

Homes were an individual and family effort. Churches and all public buildings, stores and shops were group efforts.

Today, churches are still cleaned the same way. On the pre-cleaning Sunday an invitation is issued to the entire congregation at the church service.

Response is 100 percent. This is an evening chore. And since 1932, refreshments — cookies, Amana meat specialties, coffee and soft drinks — are furnished by the local store, the meat market and the restaurants.

Brooms, Baskets

Each of the seven villages had one broom-maker, and in several of the villages there were two. Broom corn was grown from the previous year's seeds, and harvested each fall. The broom-makers produced various types of brooms for all needs in the Colonies, and also a surplus production which was sold.

Each village had a large field of willows, a special variety brought from Europe and propagated to retain flexibility. New growth was harvested and stored in a cool, damp place until needed for basket weaving.

Homestead bakery, 1920: Four-pound loaves from hearth oven.

Blacksmiths and horseshoes in 1920's.

Building an elevator in Amana.

Typical men's work: Making brick in wood-fired kilns, putting up hay, logging in the 9,570 acres of forest. Lunch was brought to the fields.

Ice

Ice was delivered twice a week, on Tuesdays and Fridays.

Ice for Amana, Middle and East was cut at the Lily Lake. Ice for Homestead was cut at a man-made ice pond. Ice for South, West and High was cut from the Iowa river.

Ice was stored in ice houses built in shady spots. Their walls were 16 inches thick, filled with sawdust for insulation. Sawdust also was placed between ice layers. The insulating worked so well that ice was always left over at the end of the season.

Harvesting ice with horses at Homestead ice pond in 1922.

Amana barnyard, 1912

Musicians play in front of brewery which once stood east of the Amana Meat Shop. Popular instruments included zithers, violins, auto-harps, mandolins, guitars.

Wine-making

Wines were made on a communal basis. Vines were planted by the Society — blue concord, red Catawba, white Niagara. The "Weinmeister" (vineyard overseer) did the necessary cultivation. Each family maintained designated rows of grapes. They tied the vines, removed excess shoots during the growing season, and pruned.

On a designated date, each family harvested its rows. The grapes were hauled to the press house, the building housing the huge press, adjacent to the "Weinkeller" or wine cellar — always the basement of the church building. There was no significance to the location; the space was available and served the purpose. Potatoes also were stored there.

Wine was distributed by punchable tickets — 20 gallons a year for men, 12 for women. Not everyone used their allotment.

When the United States voted the Prohibition Amendment and wine was discontinued in the Colonies in 1919, Amana alone poured 19,000 gallons of wine into sewers. There was a story that the next morning, every catfish between Amana and New Orleans was pleading for aspirin.

Beer, Tobacco

In early days the Amana Society operated its own breweries for beer for home consumption.

The industry was shut down when Iowa adopted prohibition in 1884, and never reopened although the laws changed from time to time until the era of national prohibition (1919-1932).

Tobacco was raised and cigars were manufactured in the community for local use.

Gathering walnuts on a family outing.

April showers brought May flowers.

Fishing above prehistoric dam of rocks laid by Indians to trap fish
in the Iowa river during low water.

Fishing at Iowa river dam in 1908.

Many families took "thresher trips". When oat harvest was completed, you hitched up a horse and wagon, packed a lunch and headed for your favorite woods spot. Each youngster holds a small bullhead by the tail.

Grapes were everywhere. They made fine wines and also beautiful background for a little boy.

Growing Up

Flowers and Currants

In the old Amana, people had flowers but not beds of just all flowers. There were trellises and grape vines and fruit trees.

This house was the kitchen house and I remember when this entire space over here was all grape vines. We used the grapes for the pies.

Other yards might have gooseberries and currants. I remember a house where they had gooseberries and currants all along the fence when we went to school, and there was a lady who lived to be over 100, and she used to watch whether we'd pick a currant. And if we picked any, she came out and told us to stop. The only flowers this lady had were a row of delphinium and some phlox.

I remember so well a little frame house in Homestead, where the lady had a large square with the corners off, and she had beautiful designs throughout. The outer border was pansies, and then came other flowers. It was right in front of her house along the sidewalk, and people always stopped and looked at that patch — it was so beautiful. — *Emma Setzer.*

Decorations in the homes once were limited to needlework, Prestele hand-colored lithographs and religious art. Walls were painted "Amana blue."

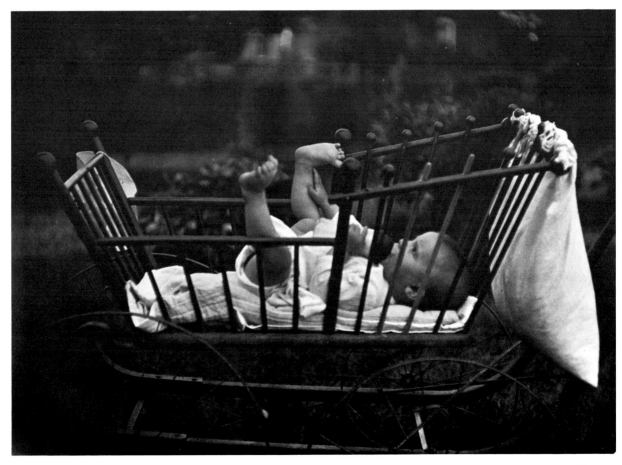

Mothers stayed home with their babies until they were two. Then mother returned to her work assignment, probably in communal kitchen, and baby went to Kinderschule.

School children shelled, cleaned and graded seed corn; picked fruit for the communal kitchens, and studied the 3 R's 5½ days a week all year. Building is the Homestead School.

School Days

At the turn of the century, spankings at school were nothing unusual. Each boy seemed to receive his share, earned or unearned. They were not too severe, but should my father learn about a spanking which I had received at school, there would follow another one at home, much more severe.

One time a boy slipped a piece of thick cardboard into the seat of his pants. It did not help much for he was caught by his big smile and perhaps by the unfamiliar sound made by the stick on the concealed cardboard.

Our conversation in and out of school was always in German. The German spoken to us and which we were taught did not contain the equivalent of "Would you care to do this?" or "Would you like to do that?" It was simply: "You do this!" or "You can do that!"

But at no time were we ever told to do something which we were not able to do, or something hazardous. If we had to climb a 20-foot ladder picking apples, our teacher always saw to it that the ladder was planted firmly and safely.

With such a prevailing spirit of being told what to do, it is not surprising that I was really never asked if I cared to take up the study of medicine. My parents merely said to me: "You will be sent to school; if you prove yourself capable and worthy, you may continue studying." And so I have continued studying ever since or at least tried to. — *Henry Moershel, M.D.*

Knitting lesson.

Girls in calico print dresses, their knitting work in baskets.

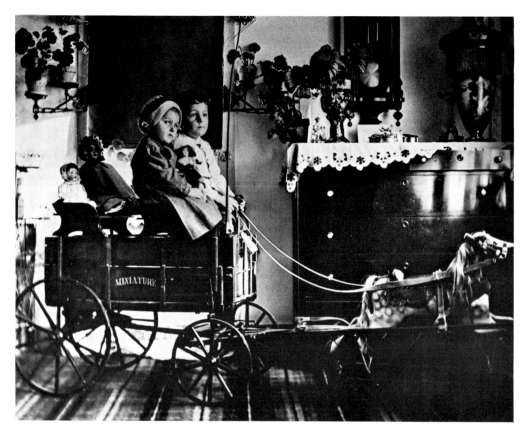

Nearly all children had hand-made hobby horses.

Schoolmates.

The Villages

Boardwalks led to homes, churches, stores, factories. Walks and fences were from native timber.

Occupations

Here are some of the trades and work assignments possible in the old Amana:

For men — Barber, basket-making, beekeeper, blacksmith, brewery, broom-maker, butcher, cabinet-maker, carpenter, cooper (maker of barrels), calico factory, flour mills, harness-maker, lumber yard, lampshade-maker, locksmith, mason, stone/brick-layer, whitewash man, machine shop, mail service (inter-village), molasses-sorgum mill, shoe-maker, saw mill, soap factory, store-keeper (general stores), main and local office staffs, tailor shops, tanneries, umbrella repair, wagon-maker, watch-maker, medical doctor, dentist, pharmacist, teacher, postmaster, railroad depot agent, farming.

For women — Kitchens, communal gardens, Kindergarten (day care centers), after-school supervisor, knitting, laundry, seamstress, woolen mills.

For boys — Harvesting apples (gathering windfalls and picking), picking cherries, etc., at communal kitchens, helping with all harvesting, agricultural activities ranging from picking potato bugs off the vines to helping harvest the large communal plantings of potatoes.

For girls — Tasks in communal kitchens such as shelling peas, pitting cherries, coring apples, etc.

Agriculture and farming — (each of the following was a separate department, staffed by specialists) working with horses, beef cattle, dairy cattle, hogs, sheep, potatoes, orchards, vineyards, winemaking.

Woolen mills (departments) — Office, raw wool, scouring and washing, dying, carding and initial yarn processing, spinning, weaving, finishing, wholesale sales and shipping, yarn rewinding.

Horse barn, Middle Amana.

Dairy herd traverses Amana street en route to the barn for afternoon milking. Square smokestack in background at right of street was part of soap factory.

The Printed Word

The printery and book bindery at Middle Amana printed forms and stationery for the stores and mills, the textbooks used in the schools, the hymn books for the churches and all other religious books.

There was no newspaper or magazine printed by the Society for circulation within the villages or outside. Many who sought to join were welcomed into the Amana Society, but no effort was made by printed materials or otherwise to recruit or convert outsiders.

All information deemed necessary for villagers was transmitted through the elders to the people at evening prayer meetings. "Personals" and other local news traveled despite the admonitions from the elders to avoid all unnecessary words.

Bees

Each village had an apiary. In East Amana it was south of the cabinet shop, and consisted of two rows of beehives separated by a path and sheltered by a grape arbor. A wooden fence surrounded it. On the grounds were several cherry trees and a large linden tree.

The apiary faced the street, and as children we were always awed and somewhat afraid of the hum of the bees as we passed by.

Sometimes during a hot, sultry day, a swarm of bees would take off from a hive and finally settle down on the branch of a nearby tree.

Then the beemaster, armed with a smoker, gloves and a veiled hat, would try to find the queen among the swarm of bees, and place her in another hive, to which the rest of the swarm would then follow.

In winter, the beehives were housed in the basement of a nearby house, which had a special little room built for them, and there they stayed until spring.

Cash

For the individual, there was no actual cash income. The Amana Society gave you a house to live in, plus certain necessary items of furniture.

There were tailor shops, sewing rooms, shoemaker shops — a shop for every necessity of life, and there was a drawing account or allowance, not in cash but in credit established for you at these shops and the general stores.

At some shops your account would be charged only with the actual cost of the raw material of the item involved, not for labor. At others, and this was extremely flexible, there was no charge. All store purchases were cost plus ten.

"Spendthrifts" would frequently overdraw their allowance. Once a year the Bruderrath, or Council of Elders, would indulge in the magnanimous gesture of "Schulden-Streichen" — erase your accumulated debts.

Customer-dictated woolen mills delivery dates ushered in a new era. To meet delivery requests, overtime was initiated — first at 15 cents an hour, then at 25 cents. As an equal opportunity gesture, farm employees were paid for husking corn, first two cents a bushel, then two and a half cents.

Then a gentleman at Detroit concocted something called the Model T. Shortly the new-fangled contraptions were chugging through Amana streets, their occupants mingling with the populace, voicing a desire for Amana craftsmanship in furniture, etc.

And although such sales were expressly and officially forbidden, the Bruderrath or Council of Elders soon "looked the other way" when woodworking, metalworking and leather crafters devoted some after-hours time to catering to private customers.

Those lacking these cash income opportunities grew and sold home-grown apples, pears, raspberries, strawberries, etc., until "Apples, Pears, Berries for Sale" signs sprouted on many Amana lawns.

All this personal and private cash income was officially frowned upon, but of necessity tolerated by the elders. — *Henry Schiff.*

Stores

The Amana General Stores, each a store-house of memories, filled to the rafters with items to treasure, to cherish, always!

The stores were built of red brick made of Amana clay, or of brown sandstone quarried at the edge of the village. Once there were horse-gnawed hitching posts outside.

Inside, at the kerosene pump, the "Kuechen-Maedels" — the junior girls of the communal kitchen staffs — replenished the kitchen supply of coal oil to light the lamps of the dining rooms and kitchens.

The basement housed barrels of vinegar and molasses. In January, there was the spicy aroma of pickled herring from barrels open for distribution among the communal kitchens.

On long counters, grocery baskets were filled with the weekly supply of coffee, tea, sugar, and spices for the kitchens, to be delivered by the "Gaeuls-Baas" or farm manager.

There were post-hole diggers and pipe lids, "Kandel-Zucker" (rock candy) and Sunday shoes, rubber boots and collar buttons, and the dress goods shelves, where in January the new "in" patterns in ginghams, shirting and dress material were viewed and the coming year's wardrobe planned.

There were spools of ribbon, black and somber, to fashion the prescribed bows on the church garb, and spools of black silk thread for tatting the dainty edging of the church cap.

On a wondrous day in early December, the Christmas candies came out — chocolate mice with string tails, chocolate rats, marshmallow bananas, and pink and white fish.

And with the years came something new, something frothy, deliciously tingling, something called soda pop. And something fantastically cold, exquisitely delicious, dipped out of five-gallon containers into something called a cone — it was ice cream. — *Henry Schiff.*

Amana before canal was relocated. Smokestack is at Woolen Mill. Building in center by canal is Colony Inn today.

Speed of Work

Historian Bertha Shambaugh wrote that the Amana man worked less rapidly than his brother in the world, but lived longer.

She told how a grain elevator burned. Because it was a busy season, enough men could not be spared to rebuild, so a nearby contractor was engaged with the understanding that available Amana masons would be employed and paid on the same terms as his own men. Mrs. Shambaugh wrote in 1908:

"In the course of a few days it was very evident that the Amana masons could not keep up with the masons of the world, and so the fair-minded superintending elder agreed that the community workmen should be paid only in proportion to the work actually done.

"With this stimulus the inspirationists set to work with a will; but while their work was unquestionably well done, the average amount accomplished and paid for was only two-thirds that of the masons from the city who had learned to labor under the influence of competition.

"An unmistakable atmosphere of industry pervades the community, but the elements of hurry and worry have largely been eliminated. To the outsider, escaping for a few days from the high pressure of the business world, Amana's ways are ways of pleasantness and all her paths are peace."

But years after the Great Change of 1932, Amana people when interviewed usually cited lack of production as a major factor in ending the communal way. The word "drones" was often heard. As far back as 1908, it was necessary to hire 175 to 200 farm hands from outside the Colonies. They were paid $125 to $175 a year plus their keep, including plenty of food and wine, and could save more than if they worked elsewhere.

Inasmuch as no money was used within the Colonies, the amounts paid for hired labor had to come from profits the Society was able to make on its industries and agriculture; the Society bought many raw materials, tools and supplies for cash, and sold many of its finished products in the outside world of commerce.

Middle Amana watch tower at top; Calico Print Factory; South Amana Meat Market in 1910 (now the Post Office and Colony Market Place).

Calico

The Amana Calico factory, which closed when World War I shut off the dyes from Germany, printed and dyed 4,500 yards every day. Amana calico, especially the "Colony Blue", sold throughout the United States and Canada at 25 cents a yard. The plant employed 25 to 30 men, of whom 10 or 12 were not colony members.

The calico designs in blue, brown and black, drew a critical eye from Amish people, who had their own ideas of "plain clothes" and considered the Amana calico a trifle worldly. Historian Bertha Shambaugh wrote:

"When the Amishman with his broad hat and buttonless coat and his gentle little wife with her purple gown come to Amana, as they frequently do, the inspection is quite mutual, for the community regard the Amish as rather queer people. Yea, verily, 'All the world is queer except thee and me, and I sometimes think thee a little queer'."

1911 winter scene: Dredge in canal in Amana.

Woolen Mill in Middle Amana.

Mill Race

The canal or mill race reaches six miles from Amana to the Iowa river at a point between South and West Amana. The water re-enters the Iowa river one mile below the Amana woolen mill.

Digging with oxen and horses and hand scrapers, work was begun May 20, 1865. In May, 1867, a dredge went into service to help complete the project.

The dredge, designed and built by Conrad Vopel, was built entirely of wood, except for the dipper or shovel, the gears, and a little steam boiler.

The mill race furnished direct water power for a woolen mill at the present site of the Amana Refrigeration, Inc., plant at Middle Amana; for the woolen mill at Amana, and for a cereal mill, a print shop for calico cloth, a starch factory, saw mills, machine shops, millwright shops and threshing machines.

Gasoline and electric motors took over from water power. Today the water turns a turbine which produces a small amount of electricity, and maintains the level of the popular lily lake, which was a slough before the canal raised its water level.

Top, foundation cave-in, old Amana Woolen Mill, Aug. 24, 1907.
Lower photo, barn fire in South Amana May 22, 1908.

Woolens

The woolen mill was already steam-powered in 1908 when Historian Bertha Shambaugh wrote that it was producing a half-million yards of flannel and ladies cloth priced from 20 to 85 cents a yard. Ten men, including seven Society members, were on the road selling.

The woolen mill employed 125, including 6 to 18 that were not Society members, and including 6 to 8 women.

Mrs. Shambaugh wrote that men working more than the required number of hours received extra compensation, sometimes in cash, sometimes in preferment of position or other special perquisites.

School boys 13 and 14 were given a try at the work. If they showed aptitude they were carefully trained. If not, they were at liberty to choose some other line of work.

"Each according to his calling or inclination is the ruling principle of industrial Amana," Mrs. Shambaugh wrote. "The natural result of such a system is intelligent and efficient workmanship."

Surveying the ruins after disastrous fire (below) which destroyed the flour and woolen mills. Fire bell sounded at noon on Saturday, Aug. 11, 1922.

Sleigh ride, winter of 1918-19.

From Oxen to Airplane

Oxen hauling water for animals in fields.

Haymaking with ox power, 1905.

Horses pulled the fire-fighters in early 1900's.

An Amana Industry, 1920. Hog powder was a conditioner manufactured and distributed by F. William Miller, Amana pharmacist, who also designed the self-feeder. Delivery by horse-drawn sled.

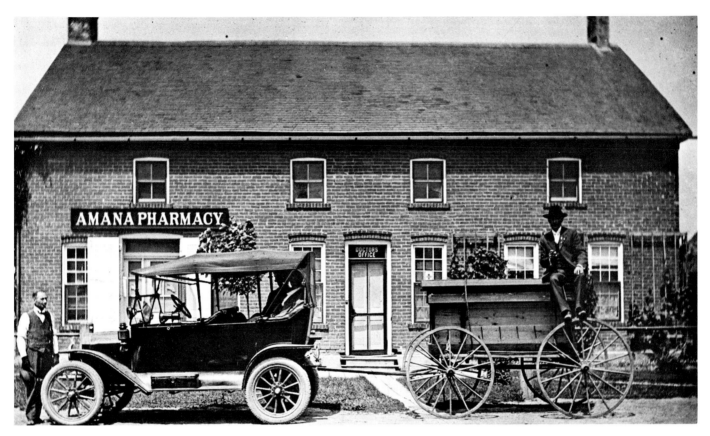

1919 photo shows early touring car with horn beside driver, tool box on runningboard. Man sits atop self-feeder for Amana hog powder, ready for delivery. At left, a load of Brunswick tires arrives for High Amana store, 1920.

Eighteen can ride as cheaply as one. An early touring car makes a big hit upon arrival at Middle Amana about 1908.

Hotels

There were four hotels. Their dates of construction: South Amana, 1862; Amana, 1872; Upper South Amana, 1874; Homestead, 1880 (burned in 1890, and rebuilt).

With a Rock Island depot at South Amana and the Milwaukee depot at Upper South, these were transfer points. Passenger trains ran once a day each direction. Hotels provided overnight lodging for persons awaiting the next train, for salesmen, early Amana "tourists" some of whom would stay as long as a week, and highway travelers with horses and wagons.

It was said that South Amana people had more English in their general conversation because of the two hotels, two railroads and the highway — it wasn't a highway then, but it was well-traveled and was even used by the Mormons.

In 1926, a new service became available. People could go from one village to another by touring car. It was a 1925 Dodge, and was chauffeured by William Sontag of Amana.

Bus brings tourists to West Amana Post Office and Store in 1921. Amana Society truck's signs and packages advertise McCormick-Deering, International Harvester, DeLaval Cream Separators and Amana Society Wool Blankets.

The air age reaches Amana. Barnstormer's bi-plane of early 1920's was photographed in a pasture near main Amana.

A New Era

People seeking beauty planted shrubs around their homes. But the elders ordered the bushes removed as too decorative for a plain, simple way of life.

Instead, the elders said, we will plant a Schulwald* of pine trees. The trees became tall and erect, and they whispered in the wind, and walking beneath their lacy boughs became one of the soft delights of communal Amana.

Time took its toll of both the communal way and the Schulwald, but visual impressions of both were recorded by the Amana photographers, working in the face of bans that were only gradually relaxed.

It is now decades since the people voted the Great Change of 1932 away from the communal life and toward more individual freedom. As the Amana people survey their heritage, they may well repeat this prayer, a favorite of the late Dr. Henry G. Moershel:

"Thanks, Heavenly Father, for this little oasis of faith and devotion serving as a sanctuary for us because of America's freedom of religion, and grant that a similar magnificent spirit of affection and sincerity be imbued and found among our young people also."

* — School woods, so named because the trees were planted by school pupils.

Children in the pine forest. At U.S. request, the trees were cut for
lumber during World War II.